The Open University

Mathematics Foundation Course Unit 8

COMPUTING I

Prepared by the Mathematics Foundation Course Team

Correspondence Text 8

The Open University Press

Open University courses provide a method of study for independent learners through an integrated teaching system including textual material, radio and television programmes and short residential courses. This text is one of a series that make up the correspondence element of the Mathematics Foundation Course.

The Open University's courses represent a new system of university level education. Much of the teaching material is still in a developmental stage. Courses and course materials are, therefore, kept continually under revision. It is intended to issue regular up-dating notes as and when the need arises, and new editions will be brought out when necessary.

Further information on Open University courses may be obtained from The Admissions Office, The Open University, P.O. Box 48, Bletchley, Buckinghamshire.

The Open University Press
Walton Hall, Bletchley, Bucks

First Published 1971
Copyright © 1971 The Open University

Printed in Great Britain by
J W Arrowsmith Ltd

SBN   335 01007 5

Contents

A Note on Studying this Text

You should study the first two sections of this unit by your normal procedure. A preliminary "read through" of section 8.3 will then complete your work on this text.

A detailed study of the third section, including working through the details of the practical work, should be taken at your own rate over about five weeks. As a guide we suggest you spend up to one hour (no more) on each of the five parts of the Programming Laboratory text, and that you use up to fifteen minutes (no more) of this time carrying through the practical work on a terminal or copying up and checking your solution on to a coding sheet.

Objectives

After working through sections 8.1 and 8.2 of this correspondence text you should have:

  (i) an understanding of the step-by-step systematic approach to problem-solving that is an essential ingredient in the process of using a computer as a problem-solving tool;
 (ii) an intuitive grasp of the nature of computation and of the problems involved in using a computer as a problem-solving tool;
(iii) an understanding of the basic concepts of computing adequate to form a basis for your computing practical work.

After a preliminary study of section 8.3 of this text you should have:

 (iv) an intuitive grasp of the functional organization of a digital computer based on an understanding of a simple conceptual model for a computer system.
  (v) an understanding of the elements of the BASIC programming language interpreted in terms of the conceptual model of the computer system.

After completing the practical work associated with the third section of this text, you should have:

 (vi) the ability to write simple programs in the BASIC programming language.

N.B.
Before working through this correspondence text, make sure you have read the general introduction to the mathematics course in the Study Guide, as this explains the philosophy underlying the whole course. You should also be familiar with the section which explains how a text is constructed and the meanings attached to the stars and other symbols in the margin, as this will help you to find your way through the text.

Structural Diagram

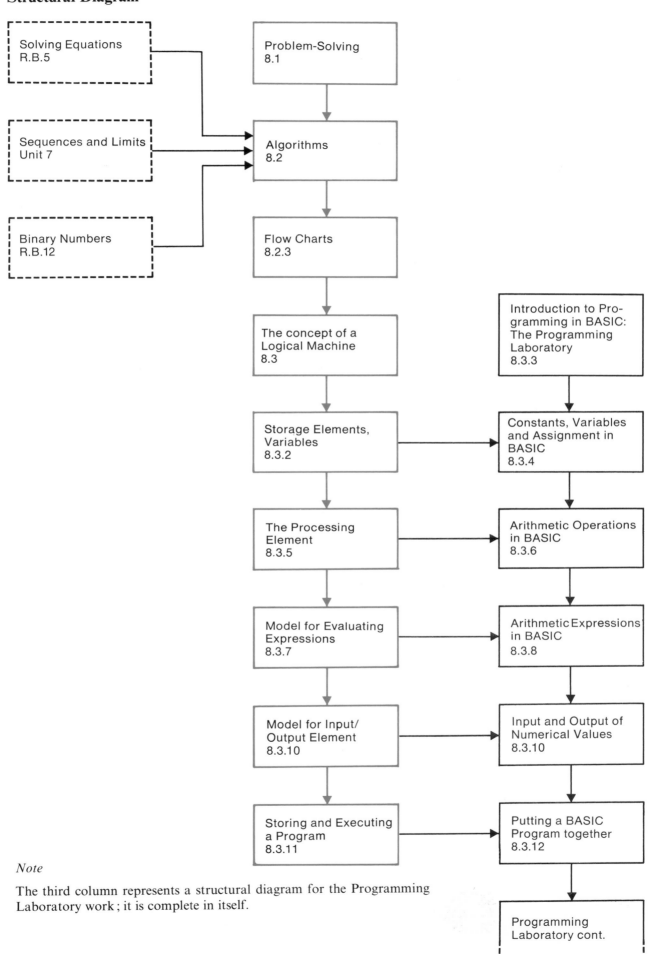

Note

The third column represents a structural diagram for the Programming Laboratory work; it is complete in itself.

Glossary

Terms which are defined in this glossary are printed in CAPITALS.

ADDRESS	The label, X, of the location holding the current value of the VARIABLE x is called the ADDRESS of the location.	23
ALGORITHM	An ALGORITHM is a PROCEDURE such that after a *finite* number of steps either a solution of the problem is obtained, or it is determined that no solution exists and execution stops.	6
BASIC	BASIC is a simple PROGRAMMING LANGUAGE used in the Foundation Course. (Beginners' All-purpose Symbolic Instruction Code.)	23
BINARY DECISION	A BINARY DECISION is a decision between *two* alternatives.	12
COMMAND	A COMMAND is a direction to a computer system which is executed immediately and does not constitute part of the stored PROGRAM.	43
CONNECTION CIRCLE	When there must be a break in a FLOW CHART a labelled CONNECTION CIRCLE is used. Two or more such symbols represent the same point in the flow chart.	13
CONSTRUCTIVE METHOD	A CONSTRUCTIVE METHOD is a PROCEDURE which enables us to construct a solution to a problem by the systematic application of a finite number of steps.	2
DECLARE A VARIABLE	To DECLARE A VARIABLE is to label a previously unlabelled STORAGE LOCATION.	22
DEVICE	A DEVICE is an apparatus capable of interpreting a sequence of INSTRUCTIONS, expressed in some LANGUAGE, which specifies the performance of certain operations by the device.	4
EXPONENT	See NORMALIZED FLOATING POINT FORMAT.	
FLOW CHART	A FLOW CHART is a pictorial representation of an ALGORITHM in which the steps to be performed are indicated by boxes with INSTRUCTIONS inside them, and the order of OPERATIONS is specified by arrows connecting the boxes.	11
INPUT BOX	In a FLOW CHART, the information which is to serve as input data to the ALGORITHM is specified in an INPUT BOX.	13
INSTRUCTIONS	INSTRUCTIONS are directions given to a DEVICE, in a LANGUAGE it can interpret, which specify the performance of certain operations by the device.	3
LANGUAGE	A LANGUAGE is a set of symbols used to convey INSTRUCTIONS to a DEVICE.	4
LINE NUMBER	A LINE NUMBER is an unsigned integer between 1 and 9999 which must appear at the beginning of each INSTRUCTION in BASIC.	44
LOGICAL MACHINE	A LOGICAL MACHINE is a machine, the design of which is based on the laws of logic — for example, an automatic computer.	1
MANTISSA	See NORMALIZED FLOATING POINT FORMAT.	

MODEL	A MODEL is a simplified representation of something, that is, an aid to visualization. For example, a set of pigeon-holes containing slips of paper is a model of a set of STORAGE LOCATIONS containing data.	1, 15, 21, 26
NORMALIZED FLOATING POINT FORMAT	NORMALIZED FLOATING POINT FORMAT is the representation of a decimal number, x, in the form $m\,E\,e$, where $x = m \times 10^e$ and $m \in [1, 10[$. m is called the MANTISSA, 10 is the base and e is called the EXPONENT.	35
OPERATIONS	OPERATIONS are processes which a DEVICE can perform.	4
OUTPUT BOX	In a FLOW CHART, the information which gives the result provided by the ALGORITHM is specified in an OUTPUT BOX.	13
PROCEDURE	A PROCEDURE for the solution of a problem, P, on a DEVICE, D, is a specification (in a LANGUAGE acceptable to D) of a sequence of discrete steps (which are performable by D) such that, if D performs the steps in the prescribed order, then a solution to P will be obtained, if one exists.	4
PROCESSING ELEMENT	The PROCESSING ELEMENT of a MODEL is a set of facilities which enables us to execute individual instructions and to trace a route through an ALGORITHM.	26
PROGRAM	A PROGRAM is a sequence of INSTRUCTIONS for execution by a computer.	23
PROGRAMMING	The task of planning and writing a series of INSTRUCTIONS to carry out some prescribed task (that is, to correspond to a particular ALGORITHM) is called PROGRAMMING.	23
PROGRAMMING LANGUAGE	A PROGRAMMING LANGUAGE is a LANGUAGE in which the INSTRUCTIONS of a PROGRAM are written.	23
STORAGE ELEMENT	The STORAGE ELEMENT in a MODEL is a collection of locations for which the model can receive and execute the following INSTRUCTIONS: (i) DECLARE A VARIABLE. (ii) Assign a value to a VARIABLE, replacing its previous value. (iii) Copy the value of a variable. (iv) Free a STORAGE LOCATION; that is, remove the label and destroy the associated value.	22
STORAGE LOCATION	A STORAGE LOCATION in a conceptual MODEL is a location in which we store the current value of some variable.	21
SUBROUTINE	A SUBROUTINE is a section of a PROGRAM which is discussed or FLOW CHARTED in detail elsewhere.	18
VARIABLE	An item of information, number, sequence, etc. being manipulated by an ALGORITHM is called a VARIABLE.	21

Bibliography

S. H. Hollingdale and G. C. Tootill, *Electronic Computers*, (Penguin Books, 1965).
Chapters 1–3 give a useful introduction to computers and computing based on a review of the history of computing.

G. Polya, *How to Solve it*, Open University Ed. (Doubleday Anchor Books, 1970).
Part I discusses problem-solving in relation to problems in mathematics. This material forms the background to our discussions on procedures and algorithms. This book is a set book for this course and you should possess a copy; it is referred to in this text as *Polya*.

R. R. Korfhage, *Logic and Algorithms: with Applications to the Computer and Information Sciences*, (John Wiley, 1966).
Chapter 5, Algorithms and Computing Machines, defines procedures and algorithms and goes on to relate these concepts to abstract machines (finite automata) and to digital computers. This material is complementary to the discussion included in the present text.

8.1   INTRODUCTION

8.1.1   Computers and Computing

Little more than two decades have elapsed since the advent of the first fully-automatic, high-speed computers; yet already they are in widespread use and they are undoubtedly destined to have a considerable influence upon the future development of many aspects of the society in which we live.

The desire to make computation less laborious has motivated the development and construction of numerous mechanical calculators as an aid to computation. The modern automatic computer represents the latest addition to a long line of calculating devices which stretches back for thousands of years to tally-sticks, sand trays and the counting-frame.

In this short course, we do not have time to discuss the history and evolution of calculating devices leading to the development of modern calculating aids and ultimately to the modern computer. However, a number of discussions suitable to the level of this course are to be found in the literature. The first book in the bibliography (Chapters 1–3) is particularly recommended as background reading if you are interested in a historical preview of the development of computing and computers.

This unit and *Unit 20, Computing II* might collectively be titled "Computer Science — An Appreciation", since our overall objective is to go some way towards providing answers to the following questions:

 (i) What is computer science?

(ii) Why is computer science important?

Before we can attempt to formulate any sort of answer to either question, we must undertake an introductory, but thorough, study of computing (as opposed to computers); that is, a study of the techniques involved in the solution of problems with the aid of a computer.

It is impossible to describe systematically those tasks which can be performed by a computer and those tasks which cannot. This is impossible for the following reasons: firstly, a computer can only perform a task which has been completely and explicitly specified by a user (so that some of the constraints on the tasks a computer can perform are directly related to the user's ability to specify the task); secondly, computers (logical machines) are the most complex of machines and we currently lack the theoretical tools necessary to analyse their activities. In this unit we shall consider both these points: the former by studying methods of specifying formally the solution to a problem; the latter by studying a simple conceptual *model* of a computer. The abstract concepts introduced in these discussions will be given concrete realization by the practical work which you will undertake in association with this and the second computing unit. Having completed the study of this text and the accompanying practical work, you should have a reasonable, intuitive grasp of the nature of computing, of the problems involved in using the computer as a problem-solving tool, and of some of the potential uses and limitations of computers.

8.1.2 Problem-solving and Constructive Mathematics

One of the useful by-products associated with any serious study of computing is that it provides an almost unrivalled opportunity for investigating two other areas of fundamental importance in mathematics, namely, problem-solving and constructive mathematics. In fact, the insight which you gain into these areas when you study computing can be almost as important as the knowledge which you gain about computing itself.

In this and the second computing unit, we shall be concerned with examining the ways in which people, with the aid of the devices at their disposal, solve problems. The advent of automatic computers (logical machines) which can manipulate very general forms of information according to a pre-specified set of instructions motivates a study of various aspects of *automatic problem-solving*. This in turn motivates detailed consideration of whole areas of problem-solving, and in particular of the problem-solving processes used in mathematics. You are recommended to read over at least Part I of *Polya** either before or after studying this unit.

By a constructive method in mathematics we mean a procedure which enables us to construct a solution to a problem by the systematic application of a finite number of steps. Up to the time of Euler (the early eighteenth century), most mathematics was not only inspired by concrete questions and problems, but also aimed to solve these problems directly by constructive techniques. As the problems increased in scope and generality, constructive techniques gradually gave way to non-constructive techniques based on pure logic. From earliest times to the advent of the modern digital computer, the speed with which man performed computations increased by a factor of perhaps 10 or 100. From the advent of the computer to the present day (about two decades) the speed with which we perform computations has increased about a million-fold. Also, we are now able to use a computer both to perform an enormous number of pre-specified individual manipulations without human intervention, and to manipulate much more complex types of information than that which can be represented by the simple concept of a number. As a consequence, the interest in constructive techniques of all types has increased enormously. This tendency will not displace (at least in mathematics) the need for logical deductive techniques; for, once we have formulated a constructive method, we wish to determine the exact conditions under which the method yields the solution of the problem under consideration. In computing, we are often reduced to judging the performance of a method on a pragmatic basis; when the method has been verified for a number of special cases and has worked satisfactorily, it is judged to be satisfactory for all similar cases. Mathematically such a procedure is unsound: we should base our judgment on logical rather than empirical evidence. Thus we must seek to prove theorems about the correctness and other relevant properties of our constructive methods. Application of logical techniques for this purpose is in its infancy as far as modern constructive methods are concerned, and the problems to be surmounted are enormous. Nevertheless, it is important that you should come to appreciate the defects and weaknesses in empirical techniques of verification of a constructive method.

* See Bibliography.

8.1.3 The Approach

In this unit, we start by considering the problems involved in describing a constructive technique as a basis for an automatic problem-solving method. We go on to examine a formal technique for describing an *algorithm* (a name for a special form of constructive method), and then to study a conceptual model for a logical machine, which provides a basis for describing the execution of an algorithm. In this final section, we also introduce the facilities available through the Student Computing Service and lay the foundations for tackling the practical computing associated with the course.

To obtain full benefit from your study of this text, we would emphasize our general recommendation for all texts: make a serious attempt at each exercise (and, if you have time, attempt each example in the text) before reading the solution provided. The experience gained in solving particular problems will help you to understand the concepts which are described in the text.

8.2 THE CONCEPT OF AN ALGORITHM

8.2.1 Method of Solution

In this section we are concerned with a particular aspect of the second phase of the activity of problem-solving distinguished by Polya in *How to Solve It*, namely, the activity of *devising a plan*. What does this activity involve? To quote Polya (page 8):

"We have a plan when we know, or know at least in outline, which calculations, computations, or constructions we have to perform in order to obtain the unknown."

In this unit we are concerned not with the whole range of techniques by which a method of solution might be obtained, but with techniques for devising a plan in a form in which it can be specified formally in terms of a set of *instructions* which a logical machine can interpret. If this goal can be achieved, then the next phase of the problem-solving activity, the phase Polya calls *carrying out the plan*, can be performed automatically by a logical machine *executing* the specified plan. When we have a formal description of a method of solution, we say that we have a *procedure* for the solution of the problem. Thus a *procedure* is a formal specification of a plan for the solution of a problem, in the sense in which Polya uses the term.

Let us consider the problem of defining more explicitly just what we mean by the concept of a *procedure*. We should first ask whether a solution exists at all. If we are given a problem and we are able to devise a plan for seeking its solution, then we may be able to decide immediately whether or not a solution exists. For example, if the existence of a solution depends on the existence of *real* roots for the quadratic equation

$$ax^2 + bx + c = 0, \qquad a, b, c \in R, \qquad a \neq 0$$

(See RB5)

then we can immediately discriminate between those cases for which a solution exists and those cases for which no solution exists, by finding the sign of the number $(b^2 - 4ac)$ for the given values of a, b, and c.

$\Big($When $b^2 - 4ac$ is positive or zero, the solution is given by the formula

$x = \dfrac{-b \pm \sqrt{b^2 - 4ac}}{2a}.\Big)$ However, things are not always as clear-cut as this; often it may be necessary to carry out part of the plan before being able to decide whether or not a solution exists. Sometimes it may not be possible to decide, on the basis of the plan devised, whether or not a solution exists. For example, if the existence of the solution depends upon the existence of the limit of a sequence (see *Unit 7, Sequences and Limits I*), then there is no general procedure which will determine whether or not a solution exists.

This leads us to define the first characteristic of a procedure:

(i) If a problem possesses a solution, then carrying out a procedure must find a solution; if, however, the problem has no solution, then a procedure may either recognize this fact or may go on indefinitely. A procedure does not terminate with an invalid solution.

The second characteristic of a procedure may be defined as follows:

(ii) A procedure must be compatible with the *device* used for carrying it out. That is to say, it must be specified in a *language* which the device can interpret and in terms of *operations* which the device can perform (execute).

For example, suppose that the problem involves the solution of an equation; then, if the device to be used for carrying out the procedure is a man equipped with pencil and paper, the procedure might depend on a simple graphical solution of the equation (such as that described in section 2.4.1 of *Unit 2, Errors and Accuracy*). However, if the device consists of a man and a desk calculator, a more sophisticated procedure can be formulated (for example, the iterative technique also described in section 2.4.1 of *Unit 2*). In these cases, the language used to describe the procedures in *Unit 2* is fairly sophisticated, since the principal processing element is a man. It is always important to consider how best to match the procedure to the capabilities of the device used to carry it out: this applies when using any logical machine.

The third characteristic of a procedure may be defined as follows:

(iii) A procedure consists of discrete steps which are to be performed in a specified order.

This characteristic is based on the assumption that the processing device operates in terms of discrete steps each of which has a definite beginning and a definite end.

These three characteristics lead us to a formal definition for a *procedure*; this definition is based upon that given in *Logic and Algorithms* by R. R. Korfhage. (See Bibliography.)

A procedure for the solution of a problem, *P*, on a device, *D*, is a description, in a language acceptable to *D*, of a sequence of discrete steps which are performable by *D*; the ordering of these steps is such that (given proper data), if *D* performs the steps in the prescribed order, a solution to *P* will be obtained, if one exists. If no solution to *P* exists then the execution of the procedure may or may not detect this fact.

Definition 1
* *

The implementation of this definition, to obtain a formally defined procedure from an informally described method of solution,* requires a thorough knowledge and understanding of both the *language* associated with the device and also the *operations* which the device is capable of performing. (The knowledge need not, however, be complete: one can use a desk machine for addition without knowing what else one can do with it.) This may become clearer to you after we have looked at an example. We shall consider a problem to which you already know the answer: how to find the meaning of an unfamiliar word.

* We use *method of solution* as an imprecise term to correspond to the precise *procedure.*

4

Example 1 **Example 1**

Of course, you know how to find the word in a dictionary — but can you say *precisely* how to do this? Can you describe the process in very simple terms, such that even a child (which will be our device) can follow it? Think about it.

First, we must assume that the child is familiar with the alphabet. Secondly, we must assume that the child has a sufficient grasp of English to understand the instructions we give him, and that he is intelligent enough to carry out these instructions correctly. (This corresponds to the *language* associated with the device and the *operations* which the device is capable of performing.) We may then arrive at something like the following:

One way of looking up a word in a dictionary word by word and page by page is to run through the dictionary from the beginning until either you reach the word you are looking for or you come to the end of the dictionary without having found it. This, in essence, is a *method of solution*. We could turn this *method of solution* into a *procedure*, in the following way:

Compare the given word with the first word in the dictionary; if they are the same, stop searching and read the meaning of the word from the dictionary. Otherwise, compare the second word in the dictionary . . . , and so on for each word in the dictionary. If the end of the dictionary is reached without the word being found, then give up and report the failure to find a meaning.

This is a perfectly valid procedure, but it is much too time consuming. What we must do to speed the process up is to skip over large numbers of words without stopping to compare each one individually with the word we are seeking. To avoid skipping over the very word we want, a little care is needed in defining when it is safe to skip. So we suggest the following alternative procedure:

Consider each letter of the given word in turn, starting with the letter at the beginning of the word, and with the dictionary open at the first page.

For each letter in turn skip forwards from wherever you have reached in the dictionary so far, until you come either to a word having that same letter in the same position as in the given word, or to a word having, in that position, a letter further on in the alphabet than the letter sought. In the latter case, go back to the word you have just skipped from, and try skipping in smaller and smaller steps, finally checking the words individually. If you still come to a word having a letter further on in the alphabet than the letter sought you may conclude that the given word is not in the dictionary. Otherwise, proceed to the next letter in the word sought, and repeat the process. Either stop when you reach the given word, and read the meaning, or stop when you run out of letters without having found it.

This procedure could be improved, but it may serve to give you some idea of the degree of care needed in specifying a procedure. ■

Discussion

The following exercise gives you a chance to try your hand at the task of constructing a procedure. The underlying problem is fairly simple; you might encounter it in any intelligence test. Given three rods, you could quickly arrange them in the form of a triangle — or else declare the task to be impossible. But you would do this by actual manipulation of the rods themselves, and you would work haphazardly, using both hands at once, rather than in the deliberate, step-by-step manner which characterizes a procedure. Furthermore, computers are not designed to push rods around, so you will have to invent some other way of tackling the problem if (as is good practice) you think of your procedure as being specified for execution on a machine (and hence not requiring intelligence or judgment to carry it out).

Exercise 1

Given the lengths of three rigid rods, devise a procedure for deciding whether or not they can form the sides of a triangle. ■

8.2.2   The Formal Definition of an Algorithm

An *algorithm* is a procedure which also possesses the following characteristics:

  (i) A solution to the problem, if one exists, is obtained after the performance of a *finite* number of discrete steps. In other words, execution of the procedure terminates if a solution exists.

It is to be understood that the number of steps performed, although finite, may be very large and, in addition, the performance of each step may be a long and complicated process if the device executing the procedure is a complicated one.

 (ii) The procedure, when executed, also solves, either initially or concurrently, the related problem: "Does the given problem have a solution?"

This leads us to define an algorithm as follows: A procedure for solving a problem, *P*, on a device, *D*, is called an algorithm for *P* on *D* if, after the performance of a *finite* number of steps, either a solution to *P* is obtained (if a solution exists) or *D* determines and reports that *P* has no solution.

Example 1

Suppose that we wish to compute the positive integer *x* which satisfies the equation $a + x = b$ for given positive integers *a* and *b*, using a device which can understand and execute the following instructions only:

  (i) add two positive integers to obtain their sum;
 (ii) compare a pair of positive integers and recognize equality of such a pair;
(iii) store the quantities involved in the calculation;
(iv) generate the successor of any positive integer in the normal sequence of integers.

We assume that the language comprehensible to the device for which the algorithm is to be specified is a modified form of the English language which is adequate to specify the operations unambiguously. ■

Example 1

Solution of Example 1

We might attempt to formulate the algorithm as follows: test each successive member of the set of positive integers, starting with the integer 1, by applying the following steps:

Step 1   Form the sum $s = a + i$, where *a* is the positive integer given in the equation and *i* is the positive integer currently under test.

Step 2   Compare the integer *s* with the given integer *b*. If they are equal, then take the value of *i* as the value for the required solution, *x*: otherwise continue testing with the next integer *i*.

These rules certainly describe a *procedure*, but do they describe an *algorithm*? Unfortunately they do not. (Consider the application of these rules to the equation $7 + x = 4$.) If the equation has no solution within the set of positive integers, then the device will go on testing indefinitely.

This difficulty can be avoided by re-writing the rules as follows:

Step 0   Compare the values of a and b; if they are equal, halt execution and report that there is no solution: otherwise continue at Step 1 below with $i = 1$.

Step 1   Form the sum $a + i$ to obtain s, and the sum $b + i$ to obtain t, where i is the positive integer under test.

Step 2   Compare the value of s and the value of b; if they are equal, then take the value of i as the value of the required solution, x: otherwise continue testing at Step 3 below.

Step 3   Compare the value of t and the value of a; if they are equal, then halt execution with no solution: otherwise continue at Step 1 above with the next value of i.

This procedure is now also an algorithm, because if there is a positive integer solution to the equation $a + x = b$, the algorithm will find it after a *finite* number of steps (recognition is by the test $s = b$): if there is no such solution, then this will be discovered in a finite number of steps either at the first step or when the test $t = a$ is satisfied. ∎

Exercise 1

Exercise 1
(2 minutes)

Without introducing either the concept of negative integers or the techniques for manipulating equations, can you change the method of solution given in Example 1 into an algorithm which will be less laborious than that given?

HINT: you may have to modify or add to the instructions which we assume that the device can understand and execute. ∎

We have defined an algorithm as a procedure that enables a device, in a finite number of steps, either to evaluate a solution to a problem or to determine that no solution exists. We wish to conclude this section by describing a method of classifying algorithms according to the number of steps which they involve. We can identify the following cases:

(i) Algorithms in which the number of steps either is fixed independently of the data or else does not exceed some absolute maximum (called an upper bound).

(ii) Algorithms for which the number of steps is related to the data on which the algorithm operates, in such a way that we can calculate from a priori considerations either the number of steps involved or an upper bound for this number.

(iii) Algorithms for which the number of steps depends on the problem, in such a way that we cannot predict any upper bound for the number of steps involved.

An example of an algorithm of the first type would be an algorithm to convert a single symbol to a code by scanning a dictionary of symbols. For example, conversion of one of the letters $A, B, C, \ldots, Z$ to the corresponding integer $1, 2, 3, \ldots, 26$ by searching the normal alphabet. In this case, 26 is an upper bound.

Example 1 (discussed above) is an example of an algorithm of the second type. Given the coefficients in the equation, we can compute the number of steps involved.

Algorithms of the third type may arise when searching an infinite set. For example, searching the set of integers for the prime number* nearest to 2^n for a given value of n. Another example would be a computational algorithm concerned with a convergent sequence (for example, the

---

* A prime number is an integer p with the property that if a and $\frac{p}{a}$ are integers, then $a = \pm 1$ or $\pm p$. For example, 1, 2, 3, 5, 7, 11, 13 are prime numbers.

(*continued on page 8*)

Solution 8.2.1.1　　　　　　　　　　　　　　　　　　　　　　

The procedure stated below depends on the following simple theorem from plane geometry:

The sum of the lengths of any two sides of a triangle is greater than the length of the third side.

Let a, b, c, denote the lengths of the three rods. The procedure can then be expressed in three steps as follows:

Step 1　Form the sum $a + b$ and denote the result by s. Compare s and c. *If s is less than or equal to c,* then we conclude that the rods cannot form a triangle and the procedure is *complete*. Otherwise:

Step 2　Form the sum $a + c$ and denote the result by t. Compare t and b. *If t is less than or equal to b,* then we conclude that the rods cannot form a triangle and the procedure is *complete*. Otherwise:

Step 3　Form the sum $b + c$ and denote the result by u. Compare u and a. *If u is less than or equal to a,* then we conclude that the rods cannot form a triangle and the procedure is *complete*. Otherwise we conclude that the rods can form the sides of a triangle and the procedure is *complete*.　■

Solution 1　　　　　　　　　　　　　　　　　　　　　　　　

A considerable simplification is achieved by first comparing the given values of a and b:

Step 1　Compare a with b. If b is greater than a, continue with Step 2 below: otherwise halt execution — the equation has no positive integer solution.

Step 2　Set i equal to 1.

Step 3　Form the sum $s = a + i$.

Step 4　Compare s with b. If they are equal, halt execution — the solution is $x = i$: otherwise return to Step 3 with the next value of i.

The first step in this algorithm requires the device to be able to tell whether one number is greater than another, which is more than requiring it to be able to tell whether two numbers are equal or not. A suitable modification of instruction (ii) in Example 1 would take care of this.　■

(*continued from page 7*)

iterative procedure for solving the equation $f(x) = 0$, described in *Unit 2*). In this case we have a criterion which any acceptable result must satisfy, and the computation continues until this criterion is satisfied. In both of these cases, provided that the arithmetic is performed precisely, we know that the process will ultimately terminate in a finite number of steps. In fact, we must be able to *prove* termination in order to be sure that we have an algorithm rather than just a procedure. Even in these circumstances we shall often not be able to predict the number of steps necessary to produce a result.

The idea that the precision of the result increases with the number of steps performed suggests that by performing an arbitrarily large number of steps any degree of precision can be achieved. As we have seen, however, (in *Unit 2*) when computing to a fixed number of decimal places, the accumulation of round-off errors restricts the precision which can be achieved. Hence we may never succeed in satisfying the termination condition despite the fact that theoretically we can prove convergence.

For this reason, algorithms of type (iii) are often converted to algorithms of type (i) by imposing an arbitrary limit on the number of steps performed. In this case we transform the problem from

"Find a solution of . . . , if one exists"

to

"Find a solution of . . . in fewer than N steps, if one exists."

Exercise 2

Formulate an algorithm of type (ii) for deciding whether a given positive integer, $p > 2$, is prime. Specify the instructions that you assume a device must be able to understand and implement in order to carry out your algorithm. ■

Exercise 3

Formulate an algorithm of type (iii) for computing $\sqrt{2}$ to an arbitrary number of decimal places on a device capable of performing addition and division. (See section 7.1.2 of *Unit 7, Sequences and Limits I*). ■

We now come to the central issue in the automation of problem-solving, namely: "What problems can be solved by algorithms?" From an intuitive point of view the answer has been provided by the formal definitions given above: "Any problem for which we can specify exactly a step-by-step systematic method of evaluating a solution in a finite number of steps". However, our definitions specify that the algorithm must be described in a language which the device can interpret, and specified in terms of instructions which the device can perform. In the next section we shall consider the problems which arise when we attempt to specify an algorithm formally, and we shall go on to consider the instructions available if the device performing the algorithm is a modern automatic digital computer.

Exercise 2
(5 minutes)

Exercise 3
(3 minutes)

Solution 2

We expect the device to be able to understand and implement the following instructions:

  I Given two integers a and b, determine whether or not a is greater than b.

 II Given a positive number a, extract the square root of a correct to one decimal place.

III Given two numbers a and b, form the quotient $\dfrac{a}{b}$.

IV Given a number a, determine whether or not a is an integer.

 V Select the next integer in the sequence: 1, 2, ...

VI Store information.

We may construct an algorithm of type (ii) as follows:

Step 1   Given p, determine $M = \sqrt{p}$ to one decimal place and store M.

Step 2   Set $m = 2$.

Step 3   Form the quotient $\dfrac{p}{m}$.

Step 4   If this quotient is an integer, report that p is not a prime and then stop: otherwise continue with Step 5 below.

Step 5   Compare m and M. If $m > M$, report that p is a prime and then stop: otherwise continue with Step 6 below.

Step 6   Select the next positive integer after the current m and give m this new value: return to Step 3.

Notice that, if we wish to reduce the abilities which are required of the device, we may do so in two ways.

Firstly, it is unnecessary for the device to be able to extract square roots. If part of the data is a number N, such that $N^2 \geqslant p$, then N can be fed into the device and used in place of M.

Secondly, we may abolish the requirement that the device can determine whether or not, for given a, b (positive integers), $a > b$. For we may simply ask the device to form all the quotients p/m as m runs from 1 to $p - 1$, and to determine whether or not each quotient is an integer.

On the other hand, if we demand that the device has greater ability, we may require that it can recognize all prime numbers less than p. Then it simply has to divide p by these numbers and to test the corresponding quotients. ■

Solution 3

The sequence given in section 7.1.2 of *Unit 7* (Newton's method for square roots) is suitable:

$$x_0 = 1 \quad \text{(say)}$$

$$x_{n+1} = \frac{1}{2}\left(x_n + \frac{2}{x_n}\right) = \frac{x_n}{2} + \frac{1}{x_n}$$

or, in other words, start with a first guess, $x_{\text{old}} = 1$, and successively replace x_{old} by the value of x_{new} calculated from the formula:

$$x_{\text{new}} = \tfrac{1}{2}x_{\text{old}} + \frac{1}{x_{\text{old}}}$$

If it is proposed to calculate $\sqrt{2}$ to an arbitrary number of decimal places, then the device executing the algorithm must be capable of performing arithmetic on arbitrarily long numbers. ■

8.2.3 The Description of an Algorithm by a Flow Chart

The description of an algorithm requires that:

(i) we have available a *language* for describing the algorithm which is acceptable to the device which is to execute the algorithm,

and

(ii) we are able to specify a number of discrete steps, in terms of instructions which the device can perform, and an ordering of these steps into a sequence, so that the performance of the instructions leads to the solution after a finite number of the steps have been performed.

The ordered steps in sequence can be regarded as the structure of the algorithm. A convenient way of communicating an algorithm from one person to another, when the algorithm to be described is "reasonably" simple, is to use what is known as a flow chart. This is a pictorial representation of the algorithm in which the various steps to be performed are indicated by boxes with instructions specified inside them, and the order in which the steps are to be executed is indicated by arrows connecting the boxes.

As an example, we shall consider an algorithm which you have already seen, namely the one described in the solution of Exercise 8.2.2.2 on page 10 ("Is p a prime?"), and express it by means of a flow chart. Even if you have never seen any kind of flow chart before, you should find it quite easy to follow this one, for the flow chart describes the algorithm clearly and unambiguously.

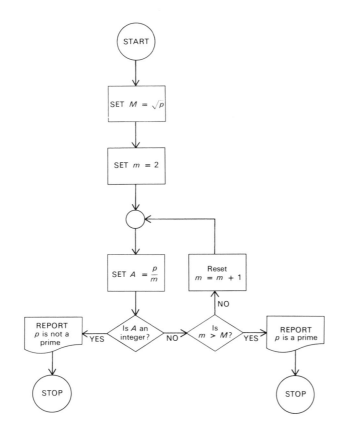

The usefulness of a flow chart for describing an algorithm is enhanced when each node (box) in the flow chart is shaped in a way which specifies the nature of the instruction to be executed at the node under consideration. The shapes are designed to convey at a glance the nature of the instructions. There is no internationally accepted standard set of shapes for these boxes, although there are a number of national standards. The shapes presented below represent commonly accepted practice. The instructions within the boxes in the flow chart are expressed in English and common mathematical and logical notation, and are only illustrative.

Initiation and Termination

Symbol   *Interpretation*

The beginning of the algorithm (that is, the point at which execution commences).

The end of the algorithm (that is, the point at which execution terminates).

Processing

Symbol   *Interpretation*

One step to be performed is specified in a rectangular box. If greater clarity is required, the processes to be performed during the execution of a single step can be broken down into sub-processes specified in several boxes. In addition, the text specifying the process may be amplified by the use of footnotes.

Binary Decisions

Symbol   *Interpretation*

The two exits to the box are labelled TRUE and FALSE, and the appropriate one is taken depending on the assertion contained in the box. Thus we choose one of two courses of action by testing the assertion.

The two exits to the box are labelled YES and NO, and the appropriate one is taken depending on the answer to the question contained in the box.

Notes

(i) Clearly these last two symbols are interchangeable, in that an assertion may be posed as a question and vice versa. The choice of the shape of box to use depends on an individual assessment of the "natural" way to present a particular decision.

(ii) More complex decision processes must be broken down into a set of simple binary decisions, that is, decisions between two possibilities as illustrated.

Connections

Symbol	Interpretation

 When it is not possible to continue a flow chart immediately after the preceding box, then a *labelled* connection circle is used. Two or more such symbols represent the same point in the flow chart, that is, the same stage in the execution of the algorithm.

 When two or more lines of flow meet (merge), the junction which they form is denoted by a connection circle. In this case the label may be omitted, unless the junction also serves as a connection in the above sense.

Communication

Symbol	Interpretation

 The information which is to serve as input data to the algorithm is specified in an input box.

 The information which forms the result provided by the algorithm is specified in an output box.

Since the average man has considerable powers of reasoning, flow charts can be expressed informally in a wide variety of formats and still be correctly interpreted. For our purposes, it is more satisfactory to restrict ourselves to the formal notation specified above, since this will help us to become accustomed to describing an algorithm in a form suitable for execution by a computer.

As a first illustration of the use of flow charts, let us look at a simple algorithm to convert a decimal integer into binary notation. We begin to specify the following algorithm in terms of instructions which an automatic device can understand and execute. Hence some of the instructions are more formal than those required for human communication.

Example 1

Describe by means of a flow chart an algorithm to convert any given decimal integer to binary form. ■

Example 1

(See RB12)

Solution of Example 1

Suppose that the given integer is n, and that the required answer is the binary number

$$b_k b_{k-1} \ldots b_2 b_1 b_0$$

where each $b_i = 0$ or 1 (for $i = 0, \ldots, k$, $k \in Z^+$). We therefore have

$$n = 2^k b_k + 2^{k-1} b_{k-1} + \cdots + 2^2 b_2 + 2 b_1 + b_0$$

from which it is evident that b_0 is the remainder when n is divided by 2. If we put

$$n = 2q_1 + b_0$$

then the quotient

$$q_1 = 2^{k-1}b_k + 2^{k-2}b_{k-1} + \cdots + 2b_2 + b_1$$

and hence b_1 is the remainder when q_1 is divided by 2. And so on . . . . In general, we shall have

$$q_i = 2q_{i+1} + b_i$$

Beginning with $q_0 = n$, we may obtain the successive b_i as the remainders upon division of the successive quotients q_i by 2. This is our algorithm for decimal to binary conversion, and we may express it by means of a flow chart as follows.

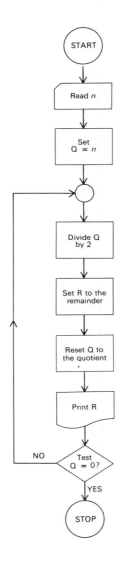

You may have noticed that our algorithm prints the binary number in the reverse order

$$b_0b_1b_2 \ldots b_{k-1}b_k \qquad \blacksquare$$

This suggests the following exercise.

Exercise 1

Draw a flow chart for an algorithm which will accept any decimal integer as input and will output the corresponding binary number with its digits arranged in the correct order. ■

Exercise 1
(5 minutes)

14

Example 2

Example 2

Given as input a single positive integer *n* and a sequence of *n* different integer values, draw a flow chart for an algorithm which will produce as output the *n* integers arranged in ascending order. ∎

Solution of Example 2

It is useful to create a simple conceptual model to help us to visualize the process which we wish to perform. Assume that we have available a set of more than *n* pigeon-holes labelled $X_1, X_2, X_3, \ldots$, each able to hold a slip of paper on which is written a number, and a note-pad which provides a source of slips for writing numbers on, and on which we can temporarily store information. We shall denote the number stored in X_i by x_i.

A simple algorithm is specified in the following flow chart. Essentially, the method adopted is to scan the pigeon-holes $X_1, X_2, X_3, \ldots$ repeatedly. During each scan, we compare the numbers in each pair of adjacent pigeon-holes in turn: if we find x_i to be greater than x_{i+1}, we interchange the contents of X_i and X_{i+1}. A tally is kept of the number of interchanges made during each complete scan. When we find a zero tally at the end of a complete scan, we know that no interchanges have been made in that scan; hence we then have $x_i \leqslant x_{i+1}$ for every adjacent pair of pigeon-holes X_i, X_{i+1}, and therefore the contents of the pigeon-holes are in ascending order.

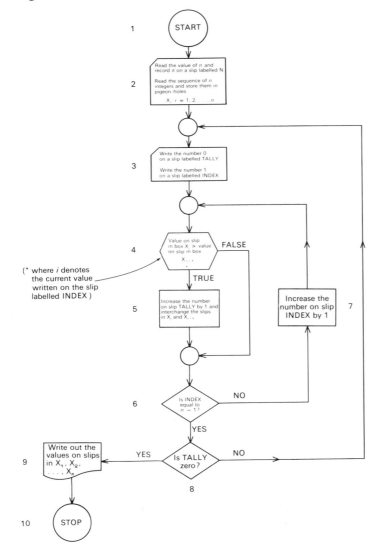

(*continued on page 16*)

15

Solution 1 **Solution 1**

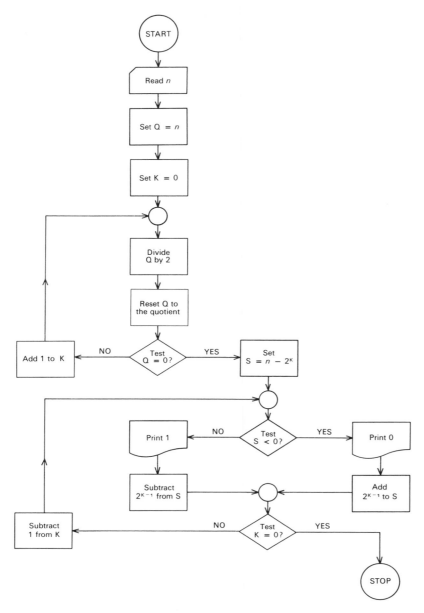

There are, of course, other solutions to this exercise.

If you have time, you could try to extend the algorithm to cope with non-integer numbers. You might also consider the reverse problem, that of binary to decimal conversion. ∎

(continued from page 15)

If you thought about this example for yourself, then you probably arrived at a different flow chart. You can verify your answer, or check the flow chart given above, by *tracing* the execution of the algorithm as follows. If each step in the algorithm is identified by labelling the corresponding box in the flow chart with the numbers 1, 2, 3, ... (note that connection boxes and junction boxes are *not* labelled, since they do not constitute separate steps in the process), then the algorithm can be traced through a table in the form shown below. For the purposes of illustration, we take $n = 5$ and work with the sequence 9, 7, 3, 4, 6.

Step Completed	Value of N	Value of TALLY	Value of INDEX	Values Contained in $X_1, X_2 \dots X_N$	Condition of Test
1					
2	5			9, 7, 3, 4, 6	
3	–	0	1	–	
4	–	–	–	–	TRUE
5	–	1	–	7, 9, 3, 4, 6	
6	–	–	–	–	NO
7	–	–	2	–	
4	–	–	–	–	TRUE
5	–	2	–	7, 3, 9, 4, 6	
6	–	–	–	–	NO
7	–	–	3	–	
4	–	–	–	–	
5	–	3	–	7, 3, 4, 9, 6	
6	–	–	–	–	NO
7	–	–	4	–	
4	–	–	–	–	TRUE
5	–	4	–	7, 3, 4, 6, 9	
6	–	–	–	–	YES
8	–	–	–	–	NO
3	–	0	1	–	

A similar sequence of interchanges will then produce the sequence 3, 4, 6, 7, 9; the subsequent scan will produce no interchanges (so that the tally value remains zero); hence the question in the decision box at Step 8 results in a YES answer; the ordered sequence is written out and the processing is terminated.

Note

A useful convention to adopt when specifying a value in a trace table is to write in the value explicitly only when it changes: this concentrates attention on those values which change at a particular step. It is also useful to distinguish between undefined values (for example, values not yet specified) and unchanged values at each step. In the table above an undefined value is indicated by a blank entry and an unchanged value by a hyphen. ∎

Exercise 2

Given as input a positive integer n and a set of n integers, draw a flow chart for an algorithm which will print out the greatest member of the set and the member of the set which has the largest absolute value. ■

The examples and exercise indicate the level of detail which must be specified for the performance of even relatively simple tasks, if each box in the flow chart contains one instruction (or question). If we continue in this way, then the flow charts specifying the algorithms for more complex tasks will become very involved, and this will reduce their usefulness. To avoid this we can extend the flow chart notation to include a symbol which can "summarize" the steps contained within a number of distinct boxes. This technique corresponds to drawing the flow chart for a hypothetical machine able to execute more complex operations than we have assumed heretofore. An example of such an extension is the subroutine concept.

Subroutines

Symbol   *Interpretation*

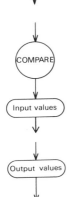

The subroutine symbol is used to indicate a subroutine, that is, a large program step which is discussed and flow charted in detail elsewhere. The text in the box specifies the name of the sub-routine and the information upon which it operates.

These symbols are used to denote the *start* and *finish* of the flow chart description of the subroutine sequence (instead of START, STOP). The start box contains the subroutine name: the finish box contains RETURN. The lozenge-shaped boxes specify the input and output values associated with the execution of the subroutine.

Example 3

Example 3

Draw a flow chart for a subroutine which accepts as input data two words (made up of a sequence of alphabetic characters) stored in the device in locations identified by A and B, and an integer T. The subroutine should produce as output the words stored in dictionary order in loca-tions A and B, and an integer which is either T, or T increased by 1 if the contents of A and B have been interchanged. Assume that the device executing the algorithm is only able to compare one pair of characters at a time, using the relations "equals", "less than" and "greater than" (which we use in place of "is the same as", "occurs earlier in the alphabet than" and "occurs later in the alphabet than" respectively). ■

Solution of Example 3

We shall use A_i to denote the ith letter of the word in location A, and similarly B_j to denote the jth letter of the word in location B. We assume that each word is stored starting at the left in each location, and that there are enough positions in A and B to store either word. Any unused positions to the right of the word are filled with blanks and we make the convention that blank is "less than" any alphabetic character. With these conventions, the words COMPUTER and COMPUTING, for example, would be stored in locations A, B as follows:

A $\boxed{\text{C}\,\text{O}\,\text{M}\,\text{P}\,\text{U}\,\text{T}\,\text{E}\,\text{R}\quad}$ B $\boxed{\text{C}\,\text{O}\,\text{M}\,\text{P}\,\text{U}\,\text{T}\,\text{I}\,\text{N}\,\text{G}\quad}$

$\quad$ i = 1 2 3 · · · · 8 9 10 $\qquad$ j = 1 2 · · · · · · 9 10

Using this model, a suitable flow chart may be drawn as follows:

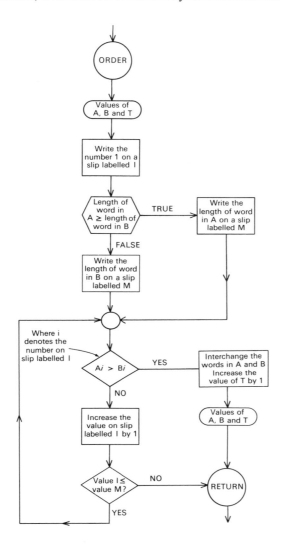

Note that the lozenge-shaped box is only used before a RETURN box to specify values which have been either set up by the subroutine or changed by the subroutine. Hence when no interchange occurs no output is specified. ■

Solution 2 **Solution 2**

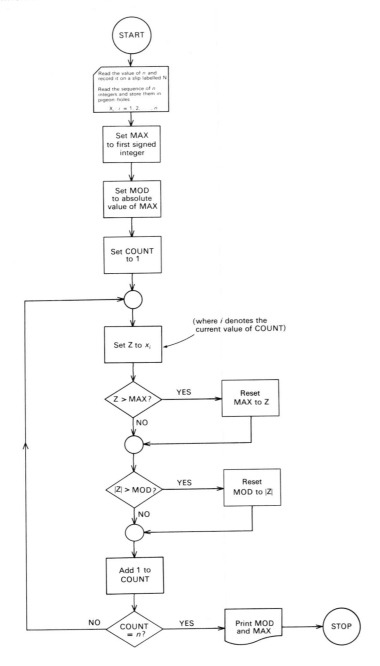

8.3   THE CONCEPT OF A LOGICAL MACHINE

8.3.0   Introduction

At the beginning of section 8.2, we stated that we were concentrating our attention on "techniques for devising a plan of solution in a form in which it can be specified formally in terms of a set of instructions which a logical machine can interpret". We called this activity "finding a *procedure* or *algorithm*". We pointed out that, if this goal can be achieved, then the next phase of the problem-solving activity (carrying out the plan or executing the algorithm) can be performed *automatically* by a logical machine. We studied briefly the problems involved in creating a formal description for an algorithm. In this section we wish to concentrate on the problems which arise when a logical machine executes an algorithm. In order to study these problems we must create a suitable, simple conceptual model for the logical machine. We shall start by examining a model machine whose prime characteristic is to be able to execute an ordered sequence of simple instructions.

The logical machine currently used for executing algorithms is the automatic digital computer; consequently we shall develop our model so that it becomes an archetype for a modern computer. This leads us to define a concise and unambiguous notation, based on the operation of our conceptual model, which can be used to describe algorithms for execution by an actual computer. These notions are discussed in relation to the process of specifying a problem for solution using the actual computer system which forms the basis of the practical work associated with the computing component of the Mathematics Foundation Course.

The model for a logical machine (computer system) which is introduced, although extremely simple, is more than adequate to form a conceptual basis for the study of the execution of algorithms and is, in fact, compatible with the structure of a modern digital computer.

8.3.1   The Concept of a Variable: the Storage Element

In section 8.2, when we discussed the execution of algorithms for sorting numbers, we introduced a model in which numbers were written on slips of paper and these slips were stored in labelled pigeon-holes. In this section we generalize this model slightly in order to provide the storage element of our computer model.

An item of information (for example, a number or sequence of letters) which is being manipulated (that is, transformed) by an algorithm is called a variable. Associated with each variable we have a name, which serves to identify the variable, and a current value which specifies the value of the variable at any particular time. Note that the value of a variable may *change* from time to time as a result of the execution of the algorithm with which it is associated. (The use of the term *variable* should be contrasted with conventional mathematical usage (see *Unit 1, Functions*.) For example, the letter x in the function specification

$$f: x \longmapsto x^2 \qquad (x \in R)$$

is a variable in the conventional mathematical sense; here it certainly has a name (the letter x) and an associated value, but this value is fixed by the subsequent declaration of the conditions which x must satisfy.)

In our conceptual model, we associate with each variable a unique location in which we can store the current value of the variable. This storage location can be visualized as a pigeon-hole in which we place a slip of paper on which is written the current value of the variable. In order to identify the variable we shall suppose that a pigeon-hole can be labelled. The assignment of labels to pigeon-holes will be a dynamic process so that the storage locations can be used over and over again when executing different algorithms. Thus we imagine the name written onto sticky tape and stuck onto the pigeon-hole holding the current value of the corresponding variable.

These ideas lead us to a formal specification for the *storage element* in our model. This definition may be summarized as follows:

The storage element in our model consists of a collection of storage locations (visualized as pigeon-holes) for which the model can receive and execute the following instructions:

Definition 3

(i) Name a currently unlabelled storage location by sticking a label over a pigeon-hole. This process is called declaring a variable. For the moment, the form which a name may take is left unspecified.

Definition 4

(ii) Assign a value to a variable by inserting a slip of paper, on which the value is written, into the appropriate storage location. This value *replaces* any existing value that may be stored in this location, so that if the location currently holds a value then this value is destroyed when a new value is assigned.

Definition 5

(iii) Copy the value of a variable by reading the value written on the slip held in the storage location associated with this variable, and writing this value onto a separate slip. In this case the slip holding the value is copied but *not destroyed*.

Definition 6

(iv) Free a storage location; that is, remove the label and destroy the associated value.

Definition 7

We shall now pause to examine how this model for the storage element of a computer system is reflected by the facilities available to the Student Computing Service.

8.3.2   Introduction to the Programming Laboratory

8.3.2

You probably know the idea behind a *language laboratory* which uses modern techniques to convey a working knowledge of a language in as short a time as possible. Our aim in the Programming Laboratory is similar, the difference being that we seek to teach a language which can be used to convey an algorithm to a computer. For this we use what is called a *programming language*.

Introduction

A computer is a highly sophisticated piece of electronic equipment; it will be sufficient, however, to base our considerations on the simple conceptual model of a computer which we are developing in this unit. Like all conceptual models, ours is an abstraction; it contains just those structural features which we need to consider in order to understand the process of constructing an algorithm in a form which can be executed by a computer. In the television programme associated with this unit, we shall develop an alternative conceptual model aimed at helping you to understand the structure and operation of the computer itself.

The Programming Laboratory texts form the basis for the computing practical work. You should work carefully through each part of the laboratory text with the aid of a computer terminal (or by posting material to be processed to the Student Computing Service). The practical details associated with the use of the Student Computing Service terminals and the Postal Service can be found in the document *The Student Computing Service Users' Guide* which has been provided.

Each part of the Programming Laboratory text is intended to be the equivalent of *one week's work on computing practicals*, which should occupy about one hour of your time (about fifteen minutes of this being spent with the computer terminal). You can work through these sections at your own rate, although you should aim to complete the five parts included in this unit during the next five weeks. You will probably find it helpful to read through the *whole* of the unit *before* tackling your first practical session.

A sequence of instructions, for execution by a computer, is called a program. (The spelling is deliberate: "program" is a technical term, and is distinct from the ordinary English word "programme".)

Definition 1
* * *

The task of planning and writing a series of instructions to carry out some prescribed task (that is, to correspond to a particular algorithm) is called programming. The language in which the instructions are written is called a programming language.

Definition 2
* *
Definition 3

We shall teach you to write programs in a simple programming language called BASIC.* (The letters stand for Beginners' All-purpose Symbolic Instruction Code — but the name itself is more indicative of the nature of the language.) The advantages of this language are that it is easy to learn and it is readily available for use on a wide variety of existing computer systems. One such computer system forms the basis for the Student Computing Service.

8.3.3 The Programming Laboratory: Part 1, Constants, Variables and Assignment

8.3.3

In section 8.3.1 we saw that a computer system incorporates a storage element which is used to store the information being handled. In our model, the computer's storage element is a collection of storage locations, each capable of holding one item of information. What constitutes an item depends upon the particular type of information involved, but certainly each storage location can hold a decimal number.

Main Text
* * *

Consider three locations within the computer's store, which have been labelled X, Y and Z (that is, variables named x, y and z have been declared) as shown in the following diagram:

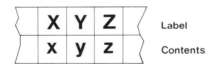

We have written the capital letter, X, above the location, in order to name the location itself, and we have written the lower case letter, x, inside the location, in order to name the contents of the location. You may not think it particularly important to be able to refer separately both to a location and to its contents, but this distinction is of fundamental importance and will help us in the subsequent discussion. The quantities X, Y, Z are labels chosen to identify the storage locations themselves and the quantities x, y, z are the current values of the variables stored in these locations. In computing jargon, the labels X, Y, Z are called the addresses of the locations.

Definition 1
* * *

In the BASIC programming language, the names of storage locations consist of either an upper case (capital) letter or an upper case letter followed by a digit; thus A7, B, M1, and W are examples of names. A storage location is allocated for each name used, and all calculations involve the current *contents* of such locations. Lower case letters are not

* BASIC was developed at Dartmouth College, New Hampshire, U.S.A. by Professor J. G. Kemeny and Professor T. E. Kurtz.

available on most input devices, so in BASIC one must always refer to variables by means of the capital letters which are the names of the corresponding locations. We shall now illustrate how this works.

In the BASIC language, numerical values may be represented in two ways, either in the form of a constant or as the contents of a specified storage location (that is, as the current value of a named variable). Constants in a program are written in the usual form for decimal numbers, except that commas, sometimes used to separate groups of three digits, are omitted (for example, 5,791 is written as 5791 in BASIC). A variable can only have a value associated with it if an item of information has been assigned to the storage location associated with this variable. In the BASIC programming language we have a notation for specifying the action of assigning a value to a variable. The assignment statement

x become 2

which corresponds to assigning the value 2 to the variable x in the location X, is written in BASIC as

LET X = 2

This command can be interpreted as

Let the contents of location X become equal to the numerical value 2

or, rather more simply, as

Let the value of X become 2

In terms of our model, the numerical value 2 is written onto a slip and this slip is stored in the location labelled X.

Notice that this statement is an *imperative* (that is, a command to carry out the stated instruction). It is important to be clear that this statement is not the same as the *equation* $x = 2$, since this is an indicative statement to be interpreted as

variable x has the value 2

or, more simply, as

x is 2.

Thus

$x = 2$

is an assertion about the existing value of x, while

LET X = 2

is an assignment of a new value to x.

Consider the execution of the instruction

LET X = 5

followed subsequently by the execution of the instruction

LET X = 9

At this point a new value, 9, is assigned to the variable named x and the old value, 5, of this variable is destroyed, since each storage location can hold only one value (item of information). Thus each new assignment to a variable *overwrites* the existing value of the variable with the new value.

When specifying the storage element in section 8.3.1, we also stated that a variable could be copied; this instruction is specified in a BASIC program by writing the name of the variable on the right-hand side of the = symbol as follows.

The instruction

LET X = Y

is interpreted as

Let the contents of location X become equal to the contents of location Y

or simply

Let the value of X become a copy of the value of Y

Consider the instructions

LET Y = Z

LET X = Y

After both commands have been executed, x, y and z will all have the same value, equal to the original value of the variable z.

Suppose, however, we execute the instructions

LET X = Y

and

LET Y = Z

Then x takes on the original value of y, and y takes on the original value of z, and these values may be different. Thus we see that the *order* in which values are assigned is of vital importance; you must therefore be careful to specify your instructions in the correct order.

Practical Exercise 1

The operational characteristics of the Student Computing Service should be studied in detail (by reading the *Users' Guide*) *before* attempting the practical work.

**Practical
Exercise 1**

You should work carefully through this exercise with pencil and paper and then process your answers on a computer terminal by means of the library program DEMON by inputting:

GET — 8DEMON

RUN

DEMON will ask for the number of the exercise, which in this case is 1, and will then request your answer. If you are using the postal service you should submit your answers neatly written on a coding sheet in the manner specified in the *Users' Guide* (just indicate the practical exercise and the relevant problem numbers with your answers) and post it to the address given in the *Users' Guide*. If you have any problems in relation to the operational aspect of the practical work you should consult the appropriate section of the *Users' Guide*.

1   Write the following numbers as BASIC constants:

  (a) 1 726   (b) $\frac{4}{5}$ (c) $\frac{2}{7}$,

  if the constants are to be stored correct to 6 significant figures.

2   Only one of the following is a valid BASIC label. Indicate whether it is (A), (B) or (C).

  (A) A3   (B) 2D   (C) PI

3   What is the value of the variable *s* after execution of the following sequence of BASIC instructions?

    LET A = 4

    LET B = 3

    LET A = B

    LET S = B

4   Write a sequence of *three* BASIC assignment instructions to interchange the values of variables currently in locations A and B. Can you achieve the same result with fewer than three instructions? ■

8.3.4   The Concept of Executing a Task: The Processing Element

The processing element of our model is a set of facilities which enables us both to execute individual instructions and to trace a route through an algorithm. The processing element may be visualized as a collection of three subhuman slaves (robots!) each able to perform a limited range of tasks. Their gross functions may be specified as follows:

 (i) The messenger: This slave's function is to transfer information from place to place. (We can imagine him to be equipped with a jotter pad on which he can record the information being transferred.)

 (ii) The calculator: This slave's function is to execute elementary instructions using the information supplied by the messenger in order to produce new items of information.

(iii) The controller: This slave's function is to interpret the instructions which specify the algorithm (we can regard this specification as a flow chart for the moment) and to delegate specific tasks to the other slaves.

It is important to remember that we are creating a conceptual model for a computer system, so that the slaves which make up the processing element must not be endowed with human characteristics; in particular, they have no memory (memory is provided by the conceptual storage element described above) and they have no intelligence or freewill. They perform a limited range of instructions with total obedience.

At this point in the creation of our model we do not want to specify in detail the full range of instructions which each of these slaves can execute, since this specification may be varied in order to create models of machines which are capable of executing instructions of varying degrees of complexity. Rather we shall examine the execution of one or two simple tasks and see just what range of functions these require of the slaves.

Let us consider the execution of the simple form of assignment instruction which we met in the previous section. Let us start from a position in which all storage locations are free (that is, unlabelled) and consider the execution of the following sequence of statements

    1   LET X = 3

    2   LET Y = X

where the integers 1, 2 are line numbers which can serve to identify the instruction being executed. The execution of these instructions can be traced by drawing up a table similar to those used earlier; in this case, however, we are concerned with putting into the table information concerning the operation of our model system. A suitable table can be arranged as follows:

Step	Action by the controller	Action by the messenger
Step 1	Recognizes an assignment instruction; starts evaluation of the value to be assigned. Copies the value onto a slip. Recognizes that the value to be assigned has now been completely evaluated. Gives the value slip to the messenger with the instruction to store it in location X.	
		Goes to the storage unit; finds no location labelled X; creates a label and labels a location X; stores the value slip in location X and returns to the controller.
Step 2	Recognizes an assignment instruction; starts evaluation of the value to be assigned. Sends messenger with the instruction to copy the value in location X.	
		Goes to the storage unit; selects location X; copies the value stored in location X onto a new slip, and returns with this value to the controller.
	Recognizes that the value to be assigned has now been completely evaluated. Gives the value slip back to the messenger with the instruction to store it in location Y.	
		Goes to the storage unit, finds no location labelled Y; creates a label and labels a location Y; stores the value slip in location Y and returns to the controller.

The sequence can be continued if there are further instructions to be executed. Notice that in the process of executing the task the controller breaks down each instruction into a carefully co-ordinated set of primitive instructions. These primitive instructions are executed sequentially (that is, one after the other in a carefully co-ordinated manner) and accordingly the internal state of our model changes in an orderly fashion. This orderly mode of operation is characteristic of modern digital computers, although in the case of a real computer system the activity accomplished by a single instruction may be very much smaller, and consequently the message transfers more numerous. This point will be brought out by the computer model which we shall examine in the TV programme associated with this unit. You should find the technique described above a useful one in helping you to understand the effect of particular instructions.

In the description given above the calculator-slave was not used during the execution of the sequence of instructions. Thus we must now consider the role that this component of the processor plays. In mathematics an *expression* is a form such as $x^2 - 4yz$; that is, it is a string, or a properly formed sequence, of variables, constants and special symbols used to denote binary operations. If our system is to be able to perform manipulations involving such expressions, then the calculator must be able to perform the basic binary operations of arithmetic on pairs of values provided by the controller.

Consider, for example, the evaluation of the expression X + Y, which is interpreted to mean $x + y$, that is, add the contents of location X to the contents of location Y. Using the tabular notation introduced above, the execution of this step can be interpreted as follows:

Step	Controller	Messenger	Calculator
Evaluate X + Y	Recognizes an arithmetic expression. Sends messenger to copy the value in X.		
		Goes to the storage unit; selects location X; copies value x on to a slip and returns.	
	Accepts the value slip and copies it on to an instruction sheet; sends messenger to copy the value in Y.		
		Goes to the storage unit; selects location Y; copies value y on to a slip and returns.	
	Accepts the value slip; copies it on to an instruction sheet and specifies the operation "add". Hands messenger the instruction sheet; sends messenger to the calculator and instructs him to wait for a reply.		
		Goes to the calculator; hands him the instruction sheet; waits for a reply.	

Step	Controller	Messenger	Calculator
			Performs the operation specified on the values provided; copies the result onto a value slip and hands it to the messenger.
		Returns with the slip to the controller.	
	Notes that the evaluation is complete.		

8.3.5 The Programming Laboratory: Part 2, Simple Arithmetic Operations

In the first part of the Programming Laboratory text we discussed constants, variables and assignment in the BASIC programming language in relation to the operation of the storage unit of our model computer system. We encountered our first instruction in the BASIC programming language: a simple assignment.

In this part of the Programming Laboratory text, we wish to develop this simple assignment instruction to incorporate the operation of the calculator component of the processing element; in particular, we consider the simple arithmetic operations performed by the calculator component.

As before, consider three locations within the storage element, labelled X, Y and Z. In BASIC we can define five arithmetic operations between pairs of storage locations, as shown in the following table:

Binary Operation	BASIC notation	Meaning
Addition	X + Y	Add the contents of location X to the contents of location Y, that is, find $x + y$.
Subtraction	X − Y	Find $x - y$.
Multiplication	X * Y	Find $x \times y$.
Division	X/Y	Find x/y.
Exponentiation	X ↑ Y	Find x^y, that is, the contents of location X raised to the power specified by the contents of location Y.

We can now attach a meaning to a statement of the form

LET Z = X + Y

for example,

let the value in Z become the value obtained by adding the contents of location X to the contents of location Y or alternatively,

> add the value of x to the value of y and place the resulting value in location Z.

We discovered in the first part of the Programming Laboratory text that constants can form the value part of a simple assignment instruction; in a similar way, a constant can replace one or both of the storage locations in a simple arithmetic operation. Thus in the table given above, either X or Y or both X and Y can be replaced by a decimal number or numbers.

Since all computations can ultimately be reduced to a sequence of simple arithmetic operations, such as we have just described, we are now in the position to write a sequence of instructions to specify the performance of an arbitrarily complex numerical computation. Before attempting some exercises, let us consider an example. What meaning can be attached to the instruction

LET X = X + 1?

We start by evaluating the expression to the right of the equality sign. Its value is obtained by copying out the value contained in location X and adding 1 to this value. The result of this calculation becomes the new value of x (that is, it is assigned to location X). Thus this instruction is to be understood as calling for the contents of location X to be increased by 1.

Summary

The operations which can be performed by our model for the processing element of a computer system are reflected by features of the BASIC programming language, and vice versa. Certain features of BASIC can be interpreted in terms of our model for the processing element as follows:

Sequential Execution: Each instruction is systematically broken down into a set of primitive instructions which can be performed by the constituent components in the processor. The BASIC instruction must specify precisely the actions to be performed.

Arithmetic Operations: A range of arithmetic operations may be applied to a pair of values, and the resultant value assigned to a storage location. This leads to an extended definition for the assignment instruction in BASIC, incorporating a simple arithmetic expression as the value to be assigned.

Practical Exercise 2

You should work carefully through this exercise with pencil and paper and then process your answers on a computer terminal by means of the library program DEMON by inputting:

GET — $\mathscr{S}$DEMON

RUN

In this case the exercise number is 2. If you are using the postal service you should submit your answers neatly written on a coding sheet in the manner specified in the *Users' Guide*.

1 Write the following mathematical expressions in BASIC notation (without parentheses):

(a) 2^b (b) xy (c) $\frac{1}{3}w$

2 Evaluate the following BASIC expressions, where $x = 13$ and $n = 3$ (giving the results to six significant figures)

(a) X * 5   (b) X ↑ N   (c) X/N

3 Assuming that initially the values in A, B, C are 2, 3 and 4 respectively, evaluate s and t by "tracing the execution" of the following sequence of BASIC instructions:

> LET S = A + C
>
> LET T = A + B
>
> LET S = T/S
>
> LET T = S ↑ 2

4 Write a sequence of BASIC instructions to evaluate a quantity x defined by the equation $\dfrac{1}{x} = \dfrac{1}{y^n} - \dfrac{1}{z^n}$ if the values of y, z and n are known. ■

8.3.6 Evaluation of Expressions

As we have seen in the previous section, the calculator element of our model processor is able to combine pairs of values by performing a range of simple arithmetic operations, and this facility allows us to define a program to evaluate an arbitrarily complex arithmetic expression. However, if programming our system is to be reasonably easy and convenient, we require a more sophisticated facility that will allow us to present arbitrarily complex arithmetic expressions in the form of a *single* instruction.

The reason why such a facility is required can be deduced from the following argument. The sequence of instructions:

> LET S = 1 − X
>
> LET T = 1 + X
>
> LET S = S／T
>
> LET E = S ↑ N
>
> LET S = 2 − Z
>
> LET T = 2 + Z
>
> LET S = S／T
>
> LET S = S ↑ M
>
> LET E = E * S

written in the notation introduced in the previous section, corresponds to evaluating e by the formula

$$e = \left(\frac{1-x}{1+x}\right)^n \times \left(\frac{2-z}{2+z}\right)^m$$

and placing the result in location E. Performing this computation by the nine simple instructions listed above has the following disadvantages:

(i) considerable clerical labour is involved, and the user has numerous opportunities to make slips;
(ii) breaking down the expression into its primitive components destroys its inherent structure and thus makes checking the specification much more difficult.

The use of a single, more complex instruction removes these problems, but requires that the user learn how to specify expressions so that the processing element can interpret them correctly. As we shall see, the single instruction correctly specified is

> LET E = (((1 − X)/(1 + X)) ↑ N) * (((2 − Z)/(2 + Z)) ↑ M)

Notice that when we shift from mathematical notation to our extended form of programming notation, six extra pairs of parentheses are introduced; if any of these parentheses are omitted then the evaluation will not be performed correctly. In order to understand how to specify a complex expression, we must consider the rules by means of which our model for the processing element evaluates expressions.

We consider first the evaluation of expressions which do not contain parentheses. In this case the *order of evaluation* is determined by a set of *rules of precedence*. You learnt such a set of rules when you were taught elementary arithmetic; the effect of rules of precedence is to determine the order in which arithmetic operations are carried out. For example, you would automatically evaluate the expression

$$4 + 3 \times 2$$

by forming the product and adding the result to 4 to give the value 10, rather than by forming the sum and multiplying the result by 2 to give 14. Thus it will be consistent with your present intuitive notions if the processing element interprets the expression

$$A + B * C$$

by forming the product of the values of variables b and c and adding the result to the value of variable a.

A complete table of the precedence rules for evaluating an arithmetic expression is given below.

Operation	BASIC notation	Meaning	Precedence
Addition	X + Y	$x + y$	Third
Subtraction	X − Y	$x - y$	Third
Multiplication	X * Y	$x \times y$	Second
Division	X/Y	x/y	Second
Taking the negative	− X	$-x$	Second
Exponentiation	X ↑ Y	x^y	First

Rules of Precedence
* * *

The variable x or the variable y, or both, may be replaced by decimal constants. In this table we have introduced one new operation (that is, one operation not included in the table given in section 8.3.5 on page 29) and this is the unary operation called *taking the negative*. This operation can be interpreted by assuming that the numerical value held in a storage location consists of a sign (+ or −) and an absolute numerical value; then the operation of taking the negative consists of changing the sign in the appropriate storage location. For example, we require that the instruction

$$\text{LET } Y = -X$$

copies the value in location X, changes the sign (of the *copy*), and stores the result as the value in location Y. (Note that the value in location X itself is *not* changed in sign.)

Using this precedence table we can define a simple rule for evaluating an arithmetic expression which contains no parentheses, as follows:

Scan the expression *from left to right* for operations of the *first level*. When you find such an operation, perform the evaluation which it specifies and resume scanning at the point where you left off. When all operations of the first level have been performed (that is, when the scan is complete), repeat the left to right scan for operations of the *second level*, and so on.

More sophisticated rules can be specified which avoid repeated scanning; however, the rule above enables us to construct, in a simple fashion, the evaluation process. Consider the following example† :

$$\text{LET } X = -A + B - C * D/E \uparrow F$$

where a, b, c, d, e and f have the values 6, 6, 5, 4, 2 and 2 respectively. The evaluation of this expression may be traced as follows:

Step	Action	Result	Comment
1	Initiate scan left to right for first level operations.		
2	Evaluate E ↑ F.	LET X = −A + B − C * D/4	First scan complete.
3	Initiate scan left to right for second level operations.		
4	Evaluate −A.	LET X = (−6) + B − C * D/4	Continue scan.
5	Evaluate C * D.	LET X = (−6) + B − 20/4	Continue scan.
6	Evaluate 20/4.	LET X = (−6) + B − 5	Second scan complete.
7	Initiate scan left to right for third level operations.		
8	Evaluate (−6) + B.	LET X = 0 − 5	Continue scan.
9	Evaluate 0 − 5.	LET X = (−5)	Third scan complete.
10	Assign the resultant value to X.		

Note

The parentheses are introduced around the negative constants to emphasize that each value consists of a sign plus an absolute value, so that the minus sign in -6, for instance, is part of the value of the constant.

The table can be interpreted in terms of the operations performed by the elements of the processor introduced in the previous section, since each evaluation involves a simple arithmetic expression incorporating a single arithmetic operation.

As you are aware, parentheses are introduced in an expression in order to indicate the order of evaluation. For example, you would automatically evaluate

$$(4 + 3) \times 2$$

to give 14 (by forming the sum before the product). The rule for evaluating expressions containing parentheses can be specified as follows:

1   Set a count to zero and scan the expression from left to right for parentheses. When a left parenthesis is encountered, increase the count by one and label the parenthesis with the current value of the count; when a right parenthesis is encountered, label it with the current value of the count, decrease the count by one and continue to scan. (The count should be zero at the end of the scan.) Record the maximum value that the count achieves.

---

† In this example, the first minus is the *unary* operation and the second minus is the *binary* operation. If the unary minus is required in the middle of an expression, it *must* be preceded by a left parenthesis.

2   A *sub-expression* is a sequence of symbols enclosed between adjacent left and right parentheses with matching labels. Evaluate the expression by applying the rule for evaluating parenthesis-free expressions to its sub-expressions, starting with the highest numbered sub-expressions first, by means of a sequence of left to right scans.   **Definition 1**

To see this rule in operation, consider the example given above:

$$\text{LET } E = (((1 - X)/(1 + X)) \uparrow N) * (((2 - Z)/(2 + Z)) \uparrow M)$$

with $x = 2$, $n = 4$, $z = 3$ and $m = 5$.

The application of the first rule produces

$$\text{LET } E = \underset{123}{(}((1 - X)\underset{33}{/}(1 + X))\underset{32}{\uparrow} N)\underset{1}{*}\underset{123}{(}((2 - Z)\underset{33}{/}(2 + Z))\underset{32}{\uparrow} M\underset{1}{)}$$

and a maximum value for the count of 3. The application of the second rule then proceeds as follows:

Step	Action	Result	Comment
1	Initiate scan for sub-expressions of order 3.		
2	Evaluate $(1 - X)$ by the rule for parenthesis-free expressions.		
3	Evaluate $1 - X$.	$\text{LET } E = \underset{12}{(}((-1)\underset{3}{/}(1 + X))\underset{32}{\uparrow} \cdots$	Continue scan.
4	Evaluate $(1 + X)$ by the rule for parenthesis-free expressions.		
5	Evaluate $1 + X$.	$\text{LET } E = \underset{12}{(}((-1)/3)\underset{2}{\uparrow} \cdots$	Continue scan.
6–9	Evaluate remaining sub-expressions of order 3.	$\text{LET } E = \underset{12}{(}((-1)/3)\underset{2}{\uparrow} N)\underset{1}{*}\underset{12}{(}((-1)/5)\underset{2}{\uparrow} M\underset{1}{)}$	End of scan.
10	Initiate scan for sub-expressions of order 2 and so on.		

8.3.7 The Programming Laboratory: Part 3, Arithmetic Expressions in BASIC

The BASIC programming language allows the user to write assignment instructions in which the value part is an arithmetic expression made up of constants, location names and arithmetic operations. These are evaluated according to the rules described in the previous section. A complete specification of, this general form of assignment instruction is given in the appropriate sections of the *Users' Guide*. As an example, consider the assignment instruction:

$$\text{LET } X = C - \underbrace{(A + D)}_{1} / \underbrace{(B \uparrow E)}_{2} * F$$

(with braces: 1 and 2 grouped under 3, then 4, then 5)

The horizontal braces show the order in which the sub-expressions are evaluated by the rules of evaluation defined in the previous section. This single BASIC instruction is equivalent to the following five simple BASIC instructions of the type discussed in Part 2 of the Programming Laboratory text:

LET P = A + D

LET Q = B ↑ E

LET R = P/Q

LET S = R * F

LET X = C − S

where P, Q, R, S are locations used as temporary storage for partial results.

If you are ever in any doubt about the precise effect of the evaluation rules on an expression, then introduce a sufficient number of additional pairs of parentheses to uniquely define the evaluation process required.

The value of a numerical variable in the BASIC programming system available to the Student Computing Service is either a finite decimal number in the approximate range 10^{-38} to 10^{+38}, or zero. (The maximum is actually 1.70141×10^{38}.) The precision of each number is six decimal digits, and each number is signed (that is, the absolute value of the variable is stored, together with an indicator defining its sign). Thus numerical values are drawn from the set of six-digit numbers defined as

$$\{x : -10^{38} \leqslant x \leqslant -10^{-38} \text{ or } x = 0 \text{ or } 10^{-38} \leqslant x \leqslant 10^{38}\}$$

In order to be able to express very large or very small numbers from this set using only six decimal digits, we need to adopt some conventions. For example, the number 86 400 000 cannot be input directly, since it contains more than 6 digits. However, this number can be written as 8.64×10^7, where 8.64 is called the *mantissa*, 10 the *base* and 7 the *exponent*. This value can be represented in BASIC as 8.64 E 7. This representation is called normalized floating point format. Normalization consists of writing the mantissa as a decimal constant in the interval [1, 10[. Normalization has the effect of making the notation unique and also of providing maximum precision, since up to six digits can be used to hold the mantissa.

The mantissa and the exponent can be held in the same storage location; the former is a signed decimal number of six digits, in the interval [1, 10[, and the latter is a signed integer between 0 and 38.

Summary

The evaluation of a complex arithmetic expression can be systematically reduced to a sequence of simple arithmetic operations which can be performed by our model for the processing element of a computer system. This facility enables us to create and interpret complex arithmetic expressions as the value part of an assignment instruction in BASIC.

The notation used to specify numerical constants in BASIC has been extended by the introduction of a notation to handle the sign of the constant and a normalized floating point format to permit the specification of both very large and very small values.

Practical Exercise 3

You should work carefully through this exercise with pencil and paper, and then process your answers on a computer terminal by means of the library program DEMON by inputting:

    GET — 𝒮DEMON
    RUN

In this case the exercise number is 3. If you are using the postal service you should submit your answers written neatly on a coding sheet in the manner specified in the *Users' Guide*.

1 Write the following mathematical constants in normalized floating point format:

(a) $-0.000\,031\,42$
(b) $14\,770\,200$
(c) 3.0091×10^{10}

2 Evaluate the value of s, in normalized floating point format, which arises from executing the following sequence of instructions:

    LET A = 5.607E − 11

    LET S = 8.372E − 9 + 3.142 * A

3 Write one or more BASIC instructions to compute the value of *y* from the formula

$$y = a + bx + cx^2 + dx^3$$

4 Apply the rules for evaluating arithmetic expressions described in section 8.3.6 to reduce the statement:

    LET X = −A + B/C + (D − E * F)↑2

to an appropriate sequence of simple assignment instructions each involving a single arithmetic operation. ■

8.3.8 Communicating with the User

So far our model computer system consists of a storage element and a processing element. However, the operations performed within these elements all take place within the computer system. You know from your experience of the Student Computing Service that it is possible to present information to a computer and to receive information from a computer, either directly, via the terminal, or indirectly by means of the coding sheets and the log sheets (the output returned to the student; see the *Users' Guide* for an appropriate description). Consequently we must add input and output elements to our model which can perform these communication functions.

Imagine that the storage and processing elements of our computer model are totally enclosed in a sealed room and that communication with the external environment takes place via two hatches constructed as shown in the diagram below:

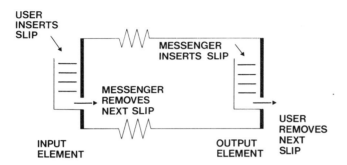

The basic operations performed on these elements are:

Input: 1 The user can stack up slips ready for input by inserting them in the input element. Each slip contains an item of information which corresponds to one line of input on the terminal or on a coding sheet.

      2 The controller can send the messenger to fetch the *next slip* from the input element.

Output: 1 The controller can send the messenger to stack up slips ready for output by inserting them in the output element. Each slip contains an item of information which corresponds to one line of output on the terminal or on a log sheet.

      2 The user can select the *next slip* from the output element.

It is important to note that these operations are *order preserving*; that is, the system accepts input slips in exactly the order in which the user provides them, and vice versa for output. As you will appreciate from using the Student Computing Service, a typical computer system can accept input and produce output in a wide variety of formats. For the purpose of our model we shall assume that the controller interprets input items and composes output items.

8.3.9 The Programming Laboratory: Part 4, Input and Output of Numerical Values

In this section we shall concentrate largely on just one aspect of the problem of communicating with a computer system, namely the problem of the input and output of numerical values under program control. Other aspects of the problem of communicating with a computer will be discussed in detail later on. We shall use the model developed in the previous section as the basis for our discussion.

When you have carefully programmed a whole sequence of steps to perform a specific calculation, you are naturally interested in displaying the result. The result will, at this stage, be held in one or more locations in the storage element so that we require an instruction to copy the value held in a storage location onto an output slip. The appropriate instruction is written in BASIC in the form

PRINT X

This statement is interpreted as follows:

Step	Controller	Messenger
1	Recognizes an output instruction; starts to assemble output information.	
	1 Sends messenger to copy the value of X.	
		Goes to storage element, selects location X, copies its value onto a slip and returns.
	2 Copies the value of X onto an output slip.	
2	Recognizes that output list is complete.	
	1 Sends messenger to place output slip in output element.	
		Goes to output element, inserts slip and returns.

Several variables may be output by a single print instruction; for instance, the instruction

PRINT X, Y, Z

will result in the production of an output slip containing the values of x, y and z printed at intervals of 15 spaces (with up to 5 print zones on one line). Each print instruction normally causes printing to commence on a new line, but if the print instruction ends with a comma, then subsequent printing will continue on the old line. The instruction

PRINT

by itself is interpreted as "line feed". If one line has just been completed, then the instructions

PRINT

PRINT X

will result in the production of two output slips, the first one blank (that is, containing a blank line), and the second containing the value of x.

One is not restricted merely to printing out the values of variables: any expression, such as might appear on the right-hand side of an assignment instruction, may appear in a print instruction; the numerical value of the entire expression will then be calculated and printed out. As a simple example, the single instruction

$$\text{PRINT } 2 \uparrow (1/3)$$

provides as output the cube root of 2 (rounded to six significant figures).

So far we have discussed printing values of variables; it is also possible to print messages or headings by writing a print instruction containing as one of the items in its print list the appropriate heading enclosed in quotation marks. For example, if x has the value 3.5, then the instruction

$$\text{PRINT ``X = '', X}$$

will result in the production of an output slip containing

$$\text{X} = 3.5$$

while the instructions

$$\text{PRINT ``X'', ``SQUARE ROOT OF X''}$$

$$\text{PRINT X, X} \uparrow (1/2)$$

will result in the production of two output slips containing

X	SQUARE ROOT OF X
3.5	1.87083

All numerical values are output correct to six significant figures. Very large numbers and very small numbers are output in normalized floating point format with a six digit mantissa.

You can arrange to input a numerical value to a variable x by writing an instruction

$$\text{INPUT X}$$

as part of your program. This instruction is interpreted as follows:

Step	Controller	Messenger
1	Recognizes an input instruction.	
	1 Sends messenger for next slip from input.	
		Goes to input unit, removes next slip and returns.
	2 Copies input value to value slip and sends messenger to assign it to location X.	
		Goes to storage element; selects location X; stores the value slip and returns.

Note that, after giving such an INPUT instruction, the user at a terminal will be prompted with a question mark (?) and he may then present any numerical constant written in BASIC format as his item of input data. The effect of the instruction is to assign a new value to x, the value

Main Text
* * *

39

to be assigned being provided by the user rather than written into a statement in the program.

The values of several variables may be input by a single instruction. Thus

INPUT X, Y, Z

will give a question mark on the terminal as a prompt and then you must provide an input item; you should type 3 numbers, separated by commas.

When there is more than one INPUT instruction in the same program you may not be quite sure what you ought to do in response to a prompt for input. The remedy is to include a PRINT instruction immediately before each INPUT instruction, which will print out some suitable message each time. The sequence of instructions:

PRINT "TYPE A VALUE FOR X"

INPUT X

will produce as output

TYPE A VALUE FOR X?

and then await the provision of an input item.

Summary

The user can inspect the results of a computation by using a PRINT instruction. Values can be input to storage locations by means of an INPUT instruction. The execution of these instructions can be interpreted in terms of a simple model for the input and output elements of the computer system.

Practical Exercise 4

Practical Exercise 4

You should work carefully through this exercise with pencil and paper and then process your answer on a computer terminal by means of the library program DEMON by inputting

GET – 𝒮DEMON

RUN

In this case the exercise number is 4. If you are using the postal service you should submit your answers neatly written on a coding sheet in the manner specified in the *Users' Guide*.

1   Write BASIC instructions to print out values of the variables *a*, *b*, *c* and *d*:

   (i) on a single line;
   (ii) in a column, one to a line;
   (iii) the values of *a* and *c* on line 1;
        lines 2 and 3 blank;
        the values of *b* and *d* on line 4.

2   Write BASIC instructions to read numerical values into the variables *a*, *b*, *c* and *d*:

   (i) one at a time, in response to individual prompts;
   (ii) all at once, in response to a single prompt.

3   Trace the execution of the following sequence of instructions:

```
INPUT A, B, C
LET S = (A + B + C)/2
LET D = (S * (S − A) * (S − B) * (S − C)) ↑ (1/2)
PRINT "SIDES OF TRIANGLE", A, B, C
PRINT "AREA OF TRIANGLE", D
```

By choosing 3, 4, 5 as a set of values for *a*, *b* and *c* respectively, illustrate the communication between the user and the system which will result from the execution of this sequence of instructions (that is, list the 3 lines of input/output as printed on the terminal log).

4 Specify the input and output resulting from the execution of the following statements, where B and H take the values 5 and 4 respectively.

PRINT "BASE, HEIGHT"

INPUT B, H

LET V = (B ↑ 2) * H/3

PRINT

PRINT "VOLUME IS", V   ■

8.3.10   The Stored Program Concept

In the model computer system which we have described above, the activity performed by the controller is specified by the sequence of instructions which he interprets. The controller interprets each instruction in turn, in the order in which the user presents them. So far we have not discussed how the user presents a complete program to the controller. A little thought will show that there are three possible ways in which this can be achieved, namely:

 (i) the user can present the program to the controller one instruction at a time through an input element (either the same one as is used for data input, or a separate one);
(ii) the user can provide the program *as a whole* to the controller as a sequence of instructions which the controller uses to determine his actions;
(iii) the user treats the program like any other piece of information associated with the problem and arranges for it to be stored in a set of storage locations.

All these techniques have been, and still are, used as means of feeding a program to a computer system. The methods are arranged in order of increasing complexity with respect to the nature of the mechanism needed to implement the technique. The first two techniques are useful, but both impose limitations, so that we shall concentrate our attention on the third technique.

We shall incorporate the third technique into our model by introducing the following additional concepts.

1 *Loading and initiating the program.*
   The user has a "buzzer" by means of which he can communicate with the controller. When he presses the buzzer the controller executes the following instructions:

   (i) Halts execution of the currently loaded program (if execution is not complete).
   (ii) Clears all information (addresses, values and instructions) from the storage element by instructing the messenger to destroy the contents of each location and to remove all the labels on the locations.
   (iii) Accepts instructions, one at a time, from the input device and places them sequentially in a set of storage locations, noting the location in which the first instruction is stored.

(iv) When the user presses the buzzer twice to signal that the end of the program has been encountered, ceases to accept instructions and initiates execution of the newly loaded program at the first instruction.

2   *Interpreting a program.*

When a program has been stored in a set of storage locations, the controller interprets the program by means of a fetch-execute cycle which can be specified as follows:

(i) Each location has an address (label) and, for simplicity, we shall assume that the set of addresses is the set of natural numbers $1, 2, 3, \ldots$. The address of a location is, of course, distinct from the variable stored in the location.

(ii) The controller keeps a record of the *address* of the instruction currently being executed (or of the first instruction while loading a program).

(iii) When the execution of the current instruction is complete the controller sends the messenger to *fetch* the next instruction (that is, the instruction in the location with address $c + 1$, where c is the contents of location C whose value is the address of the instruction just executed).

Note

We assume that each instruction can be stored completely within a single storage location.

Thus the activities of the controller may be summarized by the following flow chart:

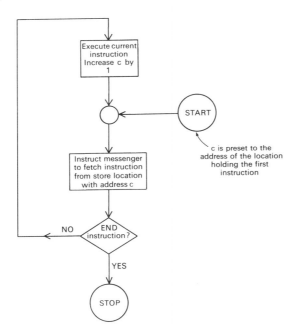

With these additions, we have specified a conceptual model for a computer system in sufficient detail to be able to construct programs. We could go on adding new concepts to increase the power and versatility of our model system in order to bring it closer to the characteristics exhibited by a modern computer system, and also to extend the range of algorithms for which we can conveniently write programs. However, we shall postpone discussion of these extensions until you have had an opportunity of using the computer system and the programming language available in the Student Computing Service. Tackling simple practical problems will provide you with a chance to study a concrete realization of the abstract principles which we have been discussing, and will help to lay the foundation on which we can build our future discussion of additional concepts. Further consideration of the stored program concept will be incorporated in the television programme associated with this unit.

8.3.11 The Programming Laboratory: Part 5, Putting a BASIC Program Together

Based on the additional concepts described above, we are now in a position to discuss the construction of a complete BASIC program.

You already know the ingredients which go to make up a simple program:

 (i) assignments of values to variables;
 (ii) input of values to variables, on demand;
 (iii) calculations, using arithmetic expressions;
 (iv) output of results.

Now we need to consider how to put these ingredients together to make an effective program.

A program consists of a sequence of instructions; in common with every other sequence, therefore, it must begin somewhere.* Although every BASIC program always begins at the beginning, in the sense that its beginning is unique, this beginning need not be the first instruction.

We introduce the concept of a BASIC *command*. A command is an instruction to the controller which is executed immediately, and does not constitute part of the stored program. Commands correspond to the buzzer in our conceptual model. One such command, presented in the form

SCRATCH

deletes the current stored program from the computer system. This command is used to get rid of the program which has been run before a completely new program is initiated.

In *Unit 7, Sequences and Limits I*, you met sequences which had no end, but you will not meet them in programming; at least, not in so far as a written program is concerned. In BASIC, the end of the program must be indicated by an explicit instruction written thus:

END

When obeyed, this instruction will bring the program to a close and print the message DONE; this instruction must occur just once in every BASIC program.

For the sake of completeness, we mention here that a program may be interrupted at any time by issuing a break command by pressing the key marked

BREAK

This action completely by-passes the BASIC system and is a direct request to the computer to terminate the current program. In general, you are advised not to use this facility except as a last resort: after such drastic action you will find it necessary to re-start the program from the beginning. The circumstances in which you should properly consider terminating a program in this abrupt manner will be discussed at a later stage.

We have so far deliberately avoided mentioning one particular feature of BASIC, since we did not wish to distract you from the fundamental

---

* "Where shall I begin, please your Majesty?" he asked. "Begin at the beginning," the King said, gravely, "and go on till you come to the end: then stop."
Lewis Carroll
Alice in Wonderland

concepts under discussion. However, in putting together a complete program, this feature becomes a fundamental issue: the principle involved is the correct ordering of the instructions which go to make up a program. What we must consider is the specification of the precise sequence in which the instructions are to be obeyed: as already hinted at, this sequence is not necessarily always the same as that in which the BASIC instructions are written.

To explain: each and every instruction in a BASIC program must begin with a unique number. This number can be any unsigned integer between 1 and 9999, and is referred to as the line number of the instruction which it precedes. No two instructions in the same program may bear the same line number: should you inadvertently type the same line number at the beginning of two or more lines, then all but the last of these lines will be ignored. Command lines do not have line numbers, since commands are not stored as part of the program.

Definition 2

An obvious idea would seem to be simply to use 1 as the line number of the first instruction typed, then 2 as the line number of the second instruction typed, and so on: if you do this, the instructions will indeed be obeyed in the order in which they are written — so why all the fuss? The point is this: the sequence in which the BASIC instructions are obeyed is determined not by the order in which they are typed and presented to the computer, but by the numerically increasing order of their line numbers. Thus, any rearrangement of the instructions of a BASIC program will in no way affect the order in which these instructions are carried out, provided only that each instruction retains its original line number. It is not suggested that you should make a habit of shuffling up the instructions of your program in an indiscriminate manner: so what is this facility really for?

The whole idea is to allow you to insert into your program, as an afterthought, instructions which you may have forgotten at an earlier stage. You may well ask how it is possible to insert another instruction between two existing instructions with line numbers (say) 17 and 18: the answer is, of course, that you cannot do so. Therefore, it is wise not to give your instructions consecutive line numbers in the first place: the BASIC system is not put out by "missing" line numbers, so it is a good idea, in the first instance, to allocate line numbers in multiples of ten. If successive instructions of your program are numbered 10, 20, 30, . . . , then there will be room for you to insert later any instructions which you may have forgotten.

Having written a program, you will naturally be anxious to try it out on the computer. The first hurdle to be overcome is that of typing out the instructions correctly on the tele-typewriter*; you must remember to press the RETURN key after typing each instruction. Spaces are ignored in the BASIC language, so it is a good idea to introduce a few judicious spaces to improve the readability of your program. Don't worry if you happen to make a mistake in typing a line: simply re-type the line correctly on the line below; this line, having the same line number, will cause the previous faulty line to be ignored.

What is the situation when you have at last correctly typed your whole program on the console? At this stage, your program will be stored in the storage unit in the computer. If you are ready to try out your program, you can cause the computer to begin obeying the instructions you have given it by presenting the command

RUN

Note that this command, like all other commands, is not part of the BASIC program and hence must not incorporate a line number. The

---

* The number zero appears as 0 on some tele-typewriters to distinguish it from the letter O.

computer will then proceed to obey your program and to print out the values requested by the print instructions in the program. If a question mark appears on the console at this stage, you must submit the items of information required by your program. When the computer reaches the end of your program it will type out the message

DONE

and await your further instructions.

All too soon, you will learn one of the harsh realities of life where programming is concerned: programs only very rarely behave as intended the first time they are run. You may be lucky with the simple programs to which you are restricted at this point in time; indeed, this is one of the main reasons for control being exercised over your progress. Nevertheless, sooner or later, you will have to face the fact that one of your carefully constructed programs just doesn't work — and that's when things begin to get interesting.

We can discount various trivial mistakes which will have been brought to your attention before you got to the stage of being able to run the program; for example, if you missed the line number from any line of your program, the computer would refuse to accept that line and would respond with an appropriate error message.

Other more explicit error messages may be printed out by the BASIC system, some before the program is run, such as

Definition 3
* *

ILLEGAL FORMAT

indicating that something is wrong with an arithmetic expression — or with the way in which an instruction is written. Such messages are signalled by the output of the word ERROR. In order to get the specific error message, indicating what is wrong, you should press any character key followed by RETURN.

Other faults may show up only when the program is actually running; not all faults are detectable by the system, but those which are detected are notified by error messages such as

DIVIDE BY ZERO — WARNING ONLY

— here, instead of actually attempting to divide by zero, the computer assumes the answer to be the largest number it can hold (roughly 1.70141 E 38) and carries on with the program.

Another error message which can be produced during program execution is

OVERFLOW — WARNING ONLY

— this occurs whenever a calculation produces a number with an absolute magnitude larger than about 1.70141 E 38.

We have given you only a few examples of the kind of error messages which you may encounter at this stage. The full list of all possible error messages from the BASIC system, together with their meanings, is given in the *Users' Guide*.

Some faults are not reported by the system and, needless to say, these are the most difficult faults to find. For example, incorrect output appears: you must then resign yourself to having to examine your program all over again in very close detail in the hope of finding out just what went wrong. In the jargon of the professional, a faulty program is said to contain one of more "bugs"; for this reason, the task of correcting a program is usually referred to as "de-bugging". This is an art which you can only really learn the hard way, but we shall do our best to help you. The first piece of advice which we are able to offer is that you should carefully annotate your programs as you write them, so that later you know exactly what you intended that they should do. At any point in a

BASIC program you may follow a line number by a remark statement, written REM, followed by any remarks which you wish to make.

You may not appreciate the need for such remarks while you are writing the program, and it is all fresh in your mind, but at some later date you will find that you need all the help you can get to help you to unravel your own program.

Assuming that you have managed to locate a fault in your program, how do you set about putting it right? If it is a case of replacing a faulty instruction, you simply type the line number of that instruction followed by the corrected version. This will cause the computer to ignore the previous incorrect version of that particular instruction. You can similarly replace any number of faulty instructions.

Should you wish to remove a particular instruction from the program, this may be accomplished by typing its line number followed by a blank line. Blank lines, like spaces, are always ignored.

If you initially allocate line numbers in multiples of ten, you will have no difficulty in inserting extra instructions between the existing instructions of your program; all you need to do is to type these extra instructions, each preceded by an appropriate line number to indicate its place in the program.

When you have corrected your program in this fashion, you may wish to see what it now looks like. If you type the command

LIST

the corrected version of your program will be printed out on the teletypewriter. If you are satisfied with it, you can try it again by once more issuing the command

RUN

You must expect to have to go through this procedure several times before your program works satisfactorily.

Let us conclude with a simple example.

Example 1

Consider the problem of determining the true interest rate per annum on a hire purchase loan.

Let c be the cost price of the goods,
   d be the down payment,
   t be the total number of payments to discharge the loan,
   p be the number of payments in one year,
and h be the total hire purchase charge.
It can be shown that the true interest rate r is given by the formula

$$r = \frac{200ph}{(c - d)(t + 1)}$$

The following sequence of instructions (printed in black) submitted on a teletype console will perform this computation. The material printed here in red will be printed out by the computer system. For example, after the instruction with line number 20 has been obeyed, the user will be prompted with a ? and should then supply the numbers 42, 8, 8. (The words printed in italics are merely explanatory and are not part of the instructions or of the print-out.)

SCRATCH   *initialize the system (command)*

10   REM...CALCULATE TRUE INTEREST RATE...

20   PRINT "COST PRICE, DEPOSIT, TOTAL H.P. CHARGE",

30   INPUT C, D, H

```
40   PRINT "PAYMENTS PER ANNUM, TOTAL NUMBER OF PAYMENTS",
50   INPUT P, T
60   REM ... INPUT DATA HAS BEEN ASSEMBLED
70   LET R = 200 * P * H/((C − D) * (T + 1))
80   REM ... TRUE INTEREST RATE HAS BEEN COMPUTED
90   PRINT "TRUE RATE OF INTEREST IS", R
100  REM ... THE COMPUTATION IS COMPLETE
110  END
```

RUN   *execute the program* (*command*)

COST PRICE, DEPOSIT, TOTAL H.P. CHARGE? 42, 8, 8

PAYMENTS PER ANNUM, TOTAL NUMBER OF PAYMENTS? 12, 12

TRUE RATE OF INTEREST IS   43.4389

DONE

       program complete (*system message*)

You will find it useful to study this example carefully before attempting the exercises given below.

Summary

In the BASIC programming language, there are commands which enable the user to assemble and execute a complete program. The execution of these commands can be interpreted in terms of a stored program concept. Our study of the BASIC system is not complete, however, since we do not yet know how to interpret the structural information in a flow chart in terms of BASIC instructions. We shall take up this problem in the next set of laboratory texts.

Practical Exercise 5

Practical Exercise 5

You should work carefully through this exercise with pencil and paper, and then either process your programs on a computer terminal or submit your programs neatly written on a coding sheet if you are using the postal service.

1 Write a complete program to accept as input data a pair of numbers and to produce as output the sum, difference, product and quotient of these numbers.

2 Write a program that will accept as input a decimal integer representing a sum of money in sterling in the form £.p and will print out the original sum and the sum converted to dollars in the form of $.¢. (Assume the exchange rate is variable.)

3 Write a program to produce the following dialogue between the user and the system

    COST PRICE?   *c*

    ANNUAL INCOME?   *i*

    SHARE YIELD   *y*

where y is calculated from the formula $y = \dfrac{100i}{c}$. The material printed in red is output; c, i, y are numerical values.

4   Correct any errors occurring in the following program where the
    values of variables c, k are computed from the value of variable f by
    the formulas, $c = \frac{5}{9}(f - 32)$, $k = c + 273$. Then trace the program
    for any value of F to obtain the corresponding values of c and k,
    and check your results by using the given formulas.

```
PRINT "FAHRENHEIT VALUE"
INPUT  F
LET  C = 5/9 * F − 32
LET  K = C + 273
PRINT  F,
PRINT  C K
```

Unit No.		Title of Text
1		Functions
2		Errors and Accuracy
3		Operations and Morphisms
4		Finite Differences
5	NO TEXT	
6		Inequalities
7		Sequences and Limits I
8		Computing I
9		Integration I
10	NO TEXT	
11		Logic I — Boolean Algebra
12		Differentiation I
13		Integration II
14		Sequences and Limits II
15		Differentiation II
16		Probability and Statistics I
17		Logic II — Proof
18		Probability and Statistics II
19		Relations
20		Computing II
21		Probability and Statistics III
22		Linear Algebra I
23		Linear Algebra II
24		Differential Equations I
25	NO TEXT	
26		Linear Algebra III
27		Complex Numbers I
28		Linear Algebra IV
29		Complex Numbers II
30		Groups I
31		Differential Equations II
32	NO TEXT	
33		Groups II
34		Number Systems
35		Topology
36		Mathematical Structures